Game Day

Behind the Scenes at a Ballpark

by Robert Young   photographs by Jerry Wachter

Carolrhoda Books, Inc./Minneapolis

For curious baseball fans everywhere.

Carolrhoda Books, Inc., c/o The Lerner Publishing Group
241 First Avenue North, Minneapolis, MN 55401 U.S.A

Website address: www.lernerbooks.com

LIBRARY OF CONGRESS CATALOGING-IN-PUBLICATION

Young, Robert
    Game Day : behind the scenes at a ballpark / by Robert Young ;
photographs by Jerry Wachter.
        p.   cm.
    Includes index.
    Summary: Describes the various activities that take place behind
the scenes before, during, and after a baseball game, using a
Baltimore Orioles game at Oriole Park at Camden Yards as an example.
    ISBN 1-57505-084-6
    1. Baseball—Juvenile literature. [1. Baseball.] I. Wachter,
Jerry, ill. II. Title.
GV867.5.Y68 1998
796.357—dc21
                                                    97-33592
Manufactured in the United States of America
1 2 3 4 5 6 – JR – 03 02 01 00 99 98

Author's Acknowledgments

Many thanks to all the people who assisted in the creation of this book: Spiro Alafassos, Brady Anderson, Richie Bancells, Rex Barney, Stacey Beckwith, Jimmy Bell, Steve Boros, Derek Britt, Butch Barnett, Darrell Carter, Leslie Evans, Jeff Garrett, Alan Gimbel, Keith Griffin, Tom Haertsch, Roland Hemond, Diane Hock, Phil Itzoe, Gordon Kennard, Frank Landrum, John Lawton, Bromley Lowe, John Maroon, Steve McCarty, Miriam McKenna, Larry Moorjani, Scott Nickle, Eddie Ridgely, Nolan Rogers, Roy Sommerhof, Kathy Townshend, Ernie Tyler, Freddy Tyler, Jimmy Tyler, Judy Valentini, Julie Wagner, Darnell Walker, Edna Weibe, Monica Windley, and Paul Zwaska.

The following organizations were very helpful to the author: Aramark, the Baltimore Orioles, the Maryland Stadium Authority, and Harry M. Stevens.

Special thanks to Tyler Young, for sparking an old interest; to Bill Stetka, for arranging interviews and answering endless questions; to Alison Schwartzwalder, Sheila West, and Matthew Lynch, for their warm hospitality; to Jerry Wachter for his willingness to take a chance; and to Sara Young, for her continued love and support.

Before the Game

It is game day. At 1:30 this afternoon, two baseball teams will play on this field. More than 45,000 people will fill these stands and cheer for their favorite team. Another 100,000 people will listen to the game on the radio. And 250,000 more will watch the game on television.

It is 6:30 a.m. on game day. The ballpark looks empty, but it is not. At the edge of the ballpark, trucks slowly roll down a ramp that leads under the field. They are making deliveries to the warehouse. Like many of the newer major league ballparks, this one has its warehouse under the field. It is a convenient place to store goods sold or used during the game. The clubhouse, where the players' lockers and the manager's office are, is also under the field.

A worker brings supplies into the warehouse under the field.

One truck delivers hot dogs to the warehouse. Another delivers napkins. Pennants and other souvenirs arrive in a third truck.

A worker uses a forklift to unload one of the trucks. Other workers load boxes of hot dogs, hamburgers, vegetables, and fresh strawberries onto stock carts. These carts will carry food and other goods to places around the ballpark where they will be needed during the game.

The smell of popcorn fills the air. Near the warehouse, the popper has begun work. His job is to make fresh popcorn for every game. He uses three large machines to pop the popcorn. Into the top of each machine he pours oil and five pounds of popcorn kernels. Then he waits.

Pop. Pop. Pop, pop. Pop, pop, pop, pop, pop. The popcorn spills out of the machines onto long metal trays. The popper pushes the popcorn back and forth over the table so that the unpopped kernels fall through small holes in the trays. He scoops the popcorn off the trays and into giant plastic bags. The popcorn from one hundred of these bags will be sold at the game today.

The bases get dirty and sometimes muddy during games, so they have to be washed before they are put in place again.

Up on the field, the grounds crew is hard at work. They have many different jobs to do. They clean the dugouts—the places where the players sit when they're not on the field during the game—and clean the bases from last night's game. They take care of the bullpens—the areas where pitchers practice throwing before entering the game—and raise the flags up the flagpoles. Working on their hands and knees, the grounds crew scrapes bubble gum off the warning track. The soft, rubberized warning track surrounds the field. When players who are running back to try to catch a ball reach the warning track, they know they are close to the fence.

The grass on the field must be mowed and watered to be ready for each game.

The grounds crew's most important job is caring for the playing field. It is their job to make sure the field is in the best condition possible. To do this, they rake the infield dirt smooth. Then they water it throughout the morning so that the ground will be firm but not hard for the game today. On a firm surface, the ball doesn't bounce so high, and it is easy and safe for the players to run and slide.

How fast a ball rolls on the field depends on how high the grass is. The higher the grass, the slower the ball will roll. At this park, the crew mows the grass so that the playing field is exactly 1¼ inches high. In the outfield, a crew member brushes fresh white paint onto the foul lines. In the infield, another worker paints the coaches' box.

Some major league baseball fields never have to be watered or mowed. These fields do not have real grass on them; they have artificial turf, which is made from plastic products.

Fields with artificial turf have their out-field lines permanently painted on. These fields don't have to be watered or mowed, but they do need a lot of care. Grounds crew workers vacuum the turf to keep it clean. They even shampoo the turf from time to time so it will look its best!

Not all the work on game day takes place at the ballpark. A short walk from the ballpark are the team offices. There's usually a lot going on at the team offices. Here, phone calls to the team—about three thousand to four thousand each day—go through the two operators. Someone wants to leave a message for a player. Another caller wonders where the best place to park is. "Any tickets left for today's game?" asks a third caller.

Down the hall from where the operators sit, the public relations office is very busy. One person uses a computer to total players' statistics, or stats. Another person helps a sportswriter arrange an interview with a player.

A member of the team's office staff gets a visit from two players.

The team mascot, known as the Oriole Bird, at work before the game

The team mascot sits in his office and answers his fan mail. The head of the production department makes final choices for the pictures that will be shown on the scoreboard and the music that will be played during today's game.

On the next floor, the general manager, or g.m., reads the results from yesterday's minor league games. If a player on one of the club's minor league teams is doing well, the g.m. might bring him up to the major league team. His job is to get the best available players on this team. Sometimes he arranges trades of players with other teams.

Ballpark scoreboards tell much more than just the score of the game. They give fans statistical information about the players. They show pictures of the players, highlights of other ball games taking place at the same time, and live camera shots of fans in the stands. Short videos are shown on the scoreboard, including games in which fans can participate. The scoreboard is also used to post important messages, such as the rules of the ballpark, and fun information, such as birthday greetings to fans of the team. The pictures and information that appear on the scoreboard are planned by the team's production department before the game and written into a script that is used by the people who control the scoreboard during the game.

A worker loads the mail at the team offices to take to the clubhouse.

Telephones are ringing in the ticket office. People are asking about tickets for today's game and for future games. Almost every single seat for today's game has been sold. Only a few are left. These tickets will go on sale an hour and a half before the game starts. A line of people hoping for these tickets has already formed outside the ticket office.

In the mail room, a worker sorts letters and packages. The team receives hundreds of pieces of mail every single day. Most of it is fan mail for the players.

A short time later, one of the clubhouse attendants drives a cart up to the team offices to pick up the mail. It takes six trips to load all the mail onto the cart. He drives it down the ramp that goes underneath the ballpark. He parks the cart outside the clubhouse and carries the mail in.

The Orioles' Cal Ripken stretches before the pre-game workout.

The clubhouse is quiet and still. The players, coaches, and manager have not come yet, but workers are getting ready for their arrival. Uniforms have to be hung up. Coffee needs to be made. Ice has to be put into the crushing machine and then into the water coolers. Bubble gum and sunflower seeds need to be set out—the team will go through a lot of these before and during the game. Letters have to be sorted into the players' mailboxes.

At around nine-thirty, the manager and the coaches begin to arrive at the ballpark. They look over the stats from yesterday and plan today's game. The manager fills out the lineup card, which tells the players' positions and batting order.

By ten-thirty, the players have started to arrive. They have work to do, too. Some will practice batting in the indoor batting cage. Others work with coaches to improve their base-running or bunting. Then there are those players who need help from the trainers. The trainers give massages, stretch players' muscles, and wrap tape around their ankles to help prevent injuries.

The players' spikes click on the concrete as they walk down the hallway toward the field in their practice uniforms. Out on the field, the grounds crew has pulled out the cage and put up the screens. The cage keeps foul balls from going into the stands. The screens help protect players in the field from balls hit while they are working on their fielding. It's time for batting practice, but not before a short warm-up on the soft outfield grass.

Players pass the time before batting and fielding practice by playing a game of hacky-sack (above). Left: Batting practice begins.

Top: *A television crew sets up one of the cameras they will use during the game broadcast.*
Bottom: *Police officers wait for their game-time assignments.*

As the players prepare for the game, so do other people around the ballpark. Television crews assemble their cameras and set them up around the ballpark. The cameras are then plugged in to thick cables that lead to the large trailer that sits under the field by the warehouse. The director will sit in the trailer and control what is shown on television during the game.

In the press box behind home plate, writers hook up their portable computers. Above them, in the broadcast booths, television and radio announcers study information about the players. In the photo pits, which are next to the dugouts, photographers set up their equipment.

Police officers gather in the seats behind home plate to receive their assignments for the game. Their job is to make sure that all the people at the game follow the rules of the ballpark and are safe.

Under the stands where the police officers are meeting is the umpire room. Here, the attendant has put out snacks and drinks for the umpires. He has polished the umpires' shoes and hung up their uniforms. Now he is preparing the baseballs for the game.

To prepare the baseballs, the attendant dips his fingers into a can of special mud that comes from the Delaware River. He rubs a light coating of the mud all over the ball. The mud takes the shine off the ball, so that it will be easier for players to see, and makes it easier to throw. About seventy baseballs will be needed for the game today.

An attendant cleans the umpires' shoes.

The place where the mud used on baseballs comes from is a well-kept secret. Here's what we do know: The mud comes from somewhere along the Delaware River, between New Jersey and Pennsylvania. Only a handful of people know exactly where to get the mud. Each year, these people take a boat to that spot and wait for the tide to go out. Then the work begins.

A man climbs overboard and shovels the mud into buckets, which are then emptied into garbage cans. It takes about eight hours of work to get the four hundred pounds of mud needed for the baseball season. A special ingredient is added to the mud to make it smooth and so that it won't stain. The mud is then put into cans and sold to major league baseball teams.

Vendors—people who sell things—begin to arrive at the ballpark. Some sell souvenirs at booths around the ballpark. They check in with a supervisor in the warehouse. After checking in, they pick up souvenirs to restock their booths.

The food vendors get ready for their day's work. Some food vendors work in the snack bars. Others carry food and drinks to people in the stands. They get to choose what food or drink they will sell each day. Vendors with the best attendance and highest sales get first choice.

A vendor at her stand

Outside the ballpark, fans are buying the last few tickets from the ticket office. Inside the ballpark, the ushers and ticket takers have arrived. At twelve o'clock sharp—an hour and a half before game time—the gates are opened, and the fans push forward. After their tickets are checked and torn, many fans rush to the seats that line the field. These seats belong to other people, but they can be used by anyone until shortly before game time. The seats that line the field are a great spot from which to see the players close up. Sometimes you can even get an autograph.

Music fills the ballpark as more fans come in. It is coming from CDs chosen by the ballpark disc jockey, who sits up above the press box in the control room. The music plays through hundreds of speakers in every part of the ballpark.

The grounds crew prepare the infield for the game.

Ushers look at tickets and help people find their seats. The visiting team takes batting and fielding practice. When they are done, the grounds crew rolls away the batting cage and takes down the screens. They smooth the infield dirt again and put down limestone powder to make the batters' boxes (where the batters will stand when they come up to bat) and the foul lines around the infield.

Both teams are in their clubhouses. The players begin to change into their game uniforms. Then they wait. Some watch television. Some answer fan mail. Some play cards. All of them think about the game that's coming up.

On some game days, the home team gives away souvenirs to fans. These fans were given posters when they arrived at the park.

It is almost game time. The umpires have finished dressing and are waiting in their room. Five minutes before the game begins, the umpires walk down the tunnel and onto the field. They meet the managers at home plate. There the managers give them each team's lineup card, and they discuss the ground rules of the ballpark. The ground rules are the special rules of each ballpark.

An announcement is made over the loudspeaker. The fans stand up, and the ballpark is suddenly quiet. Players, coaches, and managers walk to the top of the dugout steps and take off their caps. A woman stands at home plate and sings "The Star-Spangled Banner." This is a very special moment for the woman. She, along with hundreds of others, had sent a tape of her singing to the ball club. She was one of the lucky ones chosen to sing in front of all these people.

When the woman finishes singing, the crowd roars. It's time to play!

During the Game

It's the bottom of the first, and the home team is up to bat. The ball smacks into the catcher's glove. "Steee-rike!" calls the umpire. The hitter steps out of the batter's box. He looks down at the third base coach. The coach touches his cap, then his elbow. He is giving the batter a sign telling him what he's supposed to do. The sign means that the hitter is supposed to hit if the pitch looks good.

The catcher looks over at the pitching coach in the dugout. The pitching coach gives him a sign. He tells the catcher what kind of pitch he wants the pitcher to throw. The catcher relays the sign to the pitcher, and the pitcher throws a fastball.

The batter swings—crack!—and hits a long fly ball to right field. The right fielder goes back, back, back to the wall, stretches his arm as high as he can, and jumps, catching the ball in the webbing of his glove. That's the first out.

Signs are very important in baseball. They are one of the ways in which teams work together to win games. Players have to learn their team's signs and watch the coaches carefully during the game.

There are many systems for sending signs. In a simple system, when a third-base coach touches a place on his body or uniform, it tells the runners or the batter to do something. Touching the hat might mean "steal;" touching the shirt might mean "bunt." In another system, the sign doesn't count unless the coach touches something first, such as his belt. Some teams use a number system, so that when the coach touches two things, it might mean "bunt," but touching three things might mean "don't swing at the pitch."

Coaches have to be very careful about their signs because the other team is watching closely to try to figure them out. Knowing, or "stealing," the other team's signs can be a real advantage in a game.

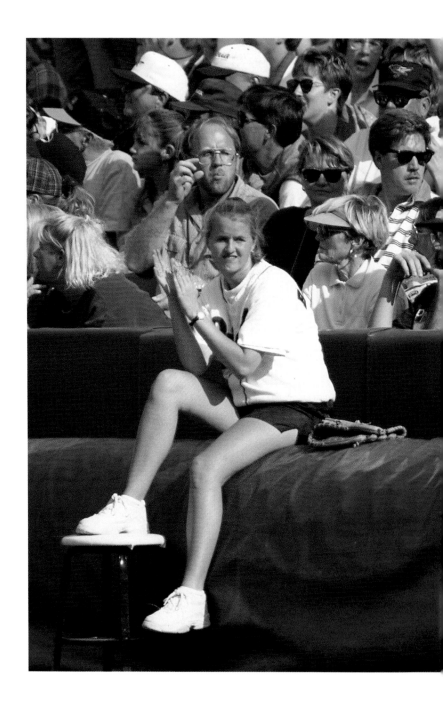

Right: *Ballgirls have mitts for catching balls that come their way.* Opposite page: *An usher takes a break to watch the game.*

Not all the good catches are made by the players. A ballgirl and ballboy sit at each end of the field. They catch ground balls that are hit into foul territory and put the balls in a bag to be re-used. In between innings, they take the balls to the ball attendant, who is sitting near the visiting team's dugout. He runs the balls out to the home plate umpire, always making sure the ump has four or five baseballs in his pockets.

The grounds crew also sits along the edge of the field. It might rain today, so they are sitting by the tarpaulin, a large, waterproof covering that has been rolled onto a long metal cylinder. If it rains hard, the crew will unroll the tarp and pull it out over the infield. The tarp will keep the infield dry so that players won't slip and risk injury.

The head groundskeeper watches the game, too. He watches from his office along the right field wall. He also keeps an eye on a computer in his office. The computer shows the latest weather information. If the weather looks bad, he can communicate that to the umpires by calling the ball attendant on his telephone.

A vendor carries soda through the stands. Fans can also buy snacks on the concourse.

"Soda here! Get your ice-cold soda here! Soda!" shouts a vendor as he walks down the steps past rows of fans. He carries twenty sodas in a metal rack with a strap that goes around his back. Tonight he will carry that rack about three miles.

When the rack is empty, the vendor hustles back to the vending room. Workers fill his rack with more sodas. A cashier gives him a ticket that shows he's taking another rack of sodas. The vendor will turn all his tickets into the cashier at the end of the game. The more soda he sells, the more money he makes.

The announcer (in yellow shirt) and reporters watch the game from the press box.

"Now batting, number 8, third baseman Cal Ripken!" The announcer's words boom throughout the ballpark. He sits in the first row of the press box and gives fans important information about the game. Next to him sits the official scorekeeper. His job is to keep track of every pitch, hit, and run. He is the person who decides if a batted ball that isn't played correctly by the team in the field is a hit or an error. Sportswriters fill the other press box seats. They keep score, take notes, and write as the game goes on.

In a broadcast booth above the press box, a radio announcer describes the game to listeners. In the next booth, television announcers comment on the game. Near them are televisions on which they can watch replays, which help them announce.

Down the hall, the control room is busy. The disc jockey pushes some buttons, and music blares from the ballpark's giant speakers. The production department chose some of the music earlier and prepared a script listing the songs to be played. Sometimes the DJ chooses the best music to fit the game at the moment.

Scoreboard operators sit in front of computers and type in information as the game is played. One person enters statistics—balls, strikes, hits, outs, runs—that are shown on the scoreboards around the ballpark. Using the production department's script, another operator types in the messages that are displayed on the huge outfield scoreboard.

In the control room, computer operators choose what fans see on the scoreboard and the television screen during the game.

Information about each player—such as how many at-bats, hits, and home runs he's had, and his batting average—along with pictures are put up on the scoreboard by an operator at another computer.

The giant television screen below the scoreboard is fun to watch. Sometimes you can even see yourself in it! A director in the control room decides what is shown on that screen. He can choose videos, replays, or live shots from cameras around the ballpark. The director has several people helping him.

On the field, the game continues. There are some good hits and more good catches. Each coach in the dugout does his best to help his team. One coach is in charge of the outfielders. He waves to direct the outfielders to different spots in the field as new batters come up. He has read information about all the batters on the other team and knows where each one is most likely to hit. Another coach helps position the players in the infield. Still another coach keeps track of every pitch thrown by the other team's pitcher. This information will help the team's hitters the next time they face that pitcher in another game.

The bullpen has a coach, too. He is in charge of the bullpen, the area beyond the fence where relief pitchers warm up. Relief pitchers fill in when the starting pitcher gets tired or starts throwing too many pitches that the opposing team can hit. If a relief pitcher is going to be needed, the pitching coach calls the bullpen coach and tells him which pitcher to get ready. The bullpen coach watches closely as the pitcher throws. Putting a new pitcher into the game before he is ready could be a disaster.

Pitchers practice throwing in the bullpen.

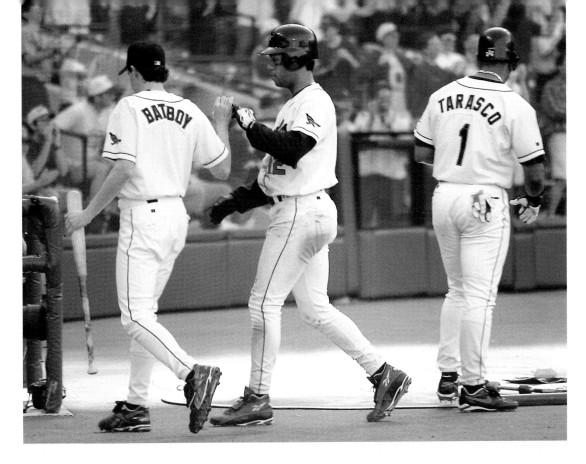

A batboy puts a player's bat away until the next time the player comes up to bat.

When the relief pitcher comes into the game, the batboy runs onto the field to get his jacket. He takes it over to the dugout so the reliever can wear it between innings to keep his throwing arm warm.

The batboy is very important to the team. His job is to make sure that the players have the right equipment so they can do their best. In addition to getting new pitchers' jackets, he makes sure each player's bat and helmet get put back where they belong after being used. The batboy also takes the players' batting gloves from them when they get on base.

Many kids would like to have the batboy's job. Because much of the job involves going into the clubhouse, where players get dressed, boys are chosen. They are usually at least sixteen years old. Some batboys get their jobs because they know someone in the team organization. Others apply for the job.

In the fifth inning, the grounds crew is back at work. When the inning is half over, crew members race onto the field, pull up the bases, and replace them with clean ones. Clean white bases are easy to see and help umpires make close calls when a player reaches a base. At the end of the inning, the crew smoothes out the infield, using rakes as well as a small tractor.

The next player at bat hits a line drive foul into the stands. It smacks off a man's hand as he tries to catch it. Owwww! The man's hand is hurt. An usher directs him to the first-aid room, which is located on the concourse (the walkway behind the stands) near the snack bars, novelty stands, and restrooms.

In the first-aid room, the nurse on duty checks the man's hand. It does not seem to be broken. But it is swollen, so she puts ice on it.

Running and sliding into bases are hard on the infield, so the grounds crew rakes the dirt smooth between innings.

Foul balls are one reason that people go to the first-aid room. Another reason is hot weather. Sitting in the stands on a hot day can make some people ill. But more people go to the first-aid room for bandages than for any other reason. The bandages are used to cover blisters people get from walking around the ballpark.

Close to the first-aid room is the police headquarters. This is the command center for the police officers who are working tonight. Sometimes people at a game break a law and have to be arrested. If they are, police bring them to this area and put them into a cell. They are kept here until they can be taken to the city jail.

Out on the concourse, people are buying food at the snack bars and team souvenirs at the novelty stands. There are television sets mounted everywhere so that people can still watch the game as they eat, shop, or walk back to their seats.

Souvenirs (top) *and soft pretzels* (bottom) *are among the many items fans can buy before and during the game.*

Up in the skyboxes, waiters bring platters of food—crab cakes, fajitas, sausages—to the people who have rented these luxury rooms. The skyboxes have tables and comfortable chairs. They have televisions, refrigerators, and sinks, too.

Televisions are also on in the clubhouse during the game. The attendants can watch the game as they work polishing the shoes that players wear for batting practice, collecting players' dirty laundry, and cleaning up.

A player jogs down the tunnel from the dugout. He is going to the video room. There he will watch a tape of his last at-bat. He wants to see what kind of pitches he got. It will help him when he comes up to bat the next time. But he has to hurry, because his team will be playing in the field soon.

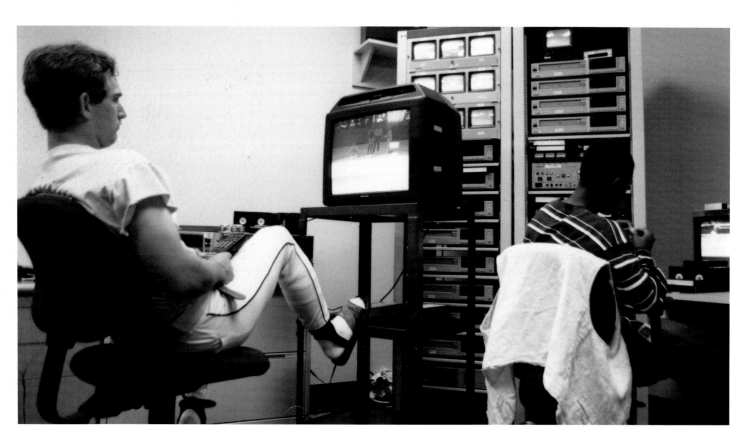

Outside the clubhouse and down the hall, young children are playing with brightly colored toys in a small room. This is the nursery, where players' wives bring their small children during the game. Here the children can play while their moms watch their dads at work.

Back on the field, the game is almost over. It is a close game, and an exciting one. The mascot stands on top of the dugout and leads the cheers for the home team. The cheers seem to work. The home team scores more runs and wins the game.

After the Game

The game is over, but game day is not. There are many more things to be done at the ballpark. A caterer has delivered food to the clubhouse for the players, and the attendants have set the food out on the tables.

As the players from the winning team shake hands, the grounds crew is already on its way to the infield. They are pushing wheelbarrows and carrying tools.

There are many jobs to do on the field. One worker pulls up the bases so they can be cleaned. Other workers fill holes dug by the spikes on the players' shoes during the game. The crew uses special metal tools to pack down the dirt.

Before the game ends, caterers help prepare food for the players to eat after the game.

Using a small shovel, a member of the grounds crew removes the limestone lines from the infield dirt.

Remember the limestone that the grounds crew used to make batters' boxes and foul lines on the infield before the game? Now that the game is over, those white lines have to be removed. If they aren't, the limestone mixes in with the infield dirt, making the color lighter. Light-colored dirt would make it hard for the grounds crew to create clear, crisp lines for the next game. So the crew use shovels to scoop up the limestone and put it into wheelbarrows. Then they rake the dirt smooth.

After all the infield dirt has been raked, workers spread small canvas tarps over two areas that need to be kept dry. They put one over the pitcher's mound. They put another over home plate and the batting area. The weather forecast doesn't call for rain, but the groundskeeper doesn't want to take chances.

As the fans slowly file out of the ballpark, food vendors are checking out of the vending rooms. They hand in the tickets that show how much they sold. The cashier in the vending room totals up their tickets and gives them each a receipt showing how much each will be paid. They'll be paid next week at the end of the team's home stand, when the team will leave town to play at other ballparks.

Snack bars are being cleaned and closed up all over the stadium. Fans crowd around the novelty stands to buy one more souvenir. Team pennants are selling well today, and so are mini-bats.

Fans leaving the ballpark are talking about the game. They're discussing their favorite plays and predicting what will happen in tomorrow's game. Down in the clubhouse, people are talking about the game too. The manager of the winning team is standing at the end of a long table. Newspaper reporters sit at the table asking questions and listening carefully to his comments. Some of the reporters scribble notes in small notebooks. Others hold out tape recorders. None of the reporters want to miss a word the manager says. They will use some of his comments in the articles they write about the game.

Fans leaving the ballpark

A player is interviewed by a television reporter in front of his locker.

When the interview with the manager is over, the reporters rush into the locker room across the hall to talk with the players. The winning pitcher is surrounded by cameras and bright lights. As reporters press microphones toward him, he politely answers every question put to him. His words will be heard on the television and radio new tonight. Other players are interviewed too, as they sit in front of their lockers.

Some of the players are not available to be interviewed. They are in the training room down the hall. Here, the trainers take care of injuries the players have gotten during the game. Trainers have to know a lot about sports injuries and how to treat them. They know which injuries are best treated with ice, and which are best treated with heat.

The trainers massage players' sore muscles and give advice on exercises that will strengthen those muscles. Strong muscles will help prevent injuries. Reporters are not allowed in the training room because the team wants information about players' health to be kept private.

After visiting the opposing team's clubhouse and doing a few more interviews, reporters take a special elevator back up to the press box. There, the public relations people give them each a page of statistics about the game. Now the reporters can write their stories about the game. They sit down at their portable computers and start writing. When they're done, they can send their articles over a modem to their newspapers.

Above the press box, the radio and television announcers are finishing their broadcasts. The TV crew shows a tape of the game highlights and the interviews that were done down in the clubhouse. The radio announcer reminds listeners about tomorrow's game, then takes calls from fans who want to discuss today's game.

The ballpark is almost empty. The police are doing a sweep—walking from section to section to make sure everyone is leaving. The TV crew is covering their cameras with plastic. Since there is a game here tomorrow, the cameras do not have to be taken down. Instead, they are wrapped in plastic in case it rains. Rain would damage this expensive equipment.

A television sportscaster wraps up his station's broadcast of the game.

Above left: *Players serve themselves a meal in the clubhouse.* Above: *A player signs autographs for fans.*

Down in the clubhouse, a few players are working out in the weight room. Some of the players, though, have showered and dressed. Many are eating from the tables set up by the clubhouse attendants. There's lots of great food to choose from—meat and fruits and vegetables and salads, even candy and ice cream! Playing baseball can sure make you hungry.

Some of the players have already left, joining their families, who have been waiting for them in the hallway outside the clubhouse. Other players begin to leave after they finish eating. They walk along the hallway that runs underneath the ballpark, past the warehouse, and up the ramp that leads outside.

There are fans waiting for them behind a metal fence. They cheer and call out the players' names. The players are tired, but some walk over to the fence to sign autographs. They sign bats and balls, hats and shirts, and baseball cards too.

It is now about seven o'clock. The coaches and the manager have gone home. So have the trainers and the players. The only people left in the clubhouse are the attendants. They have a few more hours of work to do.

First they have to clean up the dishes and food from the players' meal. Then they have to clean the whole clubhouse, picking things up and vacuuming too.

The players' uniforms have to be washed. An attendant has collected all the uniforms so they will be ready when the cleaning company comes to pick them up in a little while. The clean uniforms will be returned tomorrow at noon, in time for the next game.

Other clothing—socks and underwear—are washed at the ballpark. An attendant uses a cloth cart to collect the clothes. He wheels it down the hall to the laundry room, where there are washers and dryers. The clothes will be folded and put back into the players' lockers before the attendants leave tonight.

Back in the clubhouse, another attendant is polishing the players' game shoes. He uses a stiff wire brush to clean off the dirt. Then he uses a clear polish to make the shoes shine. When he is done, he puts the shoes back in the players' lockers. Each player's uniform number is on both of his shoes. That makes it easy to get the shoes back to the right locker.

An attendant polishes a player's shoes.

"Pickers" (above) *and "blowers"* (right) *clean the upper deck, the top tier of seats.*

Up on the field, the daylight is fading. Soon the lights on the towers above the park will be turned on. The fans have left, but the stands are not empty. A small army of workers is cleaning the ballpark.

The workers start at the top level. Forty-five "pickers" walk through each section picking up large pieces of trash. They put the trash into large garbage bags, tie the tops and put the bags out on the concourse.

The pickers are followed by another group of workers. These workers carry backpack blowers. They aim the nozzles at the ground and blow the smaller trash that the pickers did not bag up. They blow the trash to the bottom of the upper deck, then over the edge. The trash falls like snow to the second level.

When the whole upper level has been cleaned, the cleaning crew moves down to the second level. Here, they follow the same steps they did on the upper level: first pick up the big trash and put it in bags, then blow the small trash to the seats below.

When the workers reach the lowest level, the small trash is blown into the wide aisles. Then large vacuum cleaners called billy goats are used to pick up the small trash. These vacuums are also used to clean the concourses and entries into the ballpark.

A trash crew drives carts around the ballpark to pick up all the bags of garbage. They pick up about five thousand bags of trash after each game!

Above left: *The blowers have moved on to the middle tier of seats.* Above: *A worker pushes a large vacuum cleaner through the stands.*

It is getting close to midnight. The trash crew has finally finished its job. It is time to turn off the ballpark lights.

Soon it is a new day. In the early morning light, the ballpark looks empty, but it is not. Trucks slowly roll down the ramp that leads under the field. The grounds crew will be here soon. Today is another game day.

Note to Readers

From April through September, almost every day is a game day for major league baseball clubs. The game day described in this book takes place at Oriole Park at Camden Yards in Baltimore, Maryland, the home of the Baltimore Orioles. Other teams' game days will be similar, though not identical, to the one shown here.